D1266349

EVERYDAY SCIENCE

Life Cycles

To my granddaughter, Megan Kate

Please visit our web site at: www.garethstevens.com
For a free color catalog describing Gareth Stevens Publishing's list of
high-quality books and multimedia programs, call 1-800-542-2595 (USA)
or 1-800-387-3178 (Canada). Gareth Stevens Publishing's fax: (414) 332-3567.

Library of Congress Cataloging-in-Publication Data

Riley, Peter D.
    Life cycles / by Peter Riley. — North American ed.
       p. cm. — (Everyday science)
    Summary: Introduces the concept that all living things go through stages that
together are known as a life cycle.
    Includes bibliographical references and index.
    ISBN 0-8368-3716-9 (lib. bdg.)
    1. Life cycles (Biology)—Juvenile literature. [1. Life cycles (Biology)] I. Title.
QH501.R56 2003
517.8—dc21   2003042730

This North American edition first published in 2004 by
Gareth Stevens Publishing
A World Almanac Education Group Company
330 West Olive Street, Suite 100
Milwaukee, Wisconsin 53212 USA

Original text © 2003 by Peter Riley. Images © 2003 by Franklin Watts.
First published in 2003 by Franklin Watts, 96 Leonard Street, London, EC2A 4XD, England.
This U.S. edition copyright © 2004 by Gareth Stevens, Inc.

Series Editor: Sarah Peutrill
Designer: Ian Thompson
Photography: Ray Moller (unless otherwise credited)
Photo Researcher: Diana Morris
Gareth Stevens Editor: Carol Ryback
Gareth Stevens Designer: Melissa Valuch

Picture Credits: (t) top, (b) bottom, (c) center, (l) left, (r) right
Corbis: p. 24(l); /Pat Doyle, p. 23(cr); /Eric and David Hosking, p. 21; /Lynda Richardson, p. 20(t); /Roger Tidman, p. 20(b).
Ecoscene/Papilio: /Frank Blackburn, p. 27(cr); /Paul Franklin, front cover and pp. 16(b), 18(b); /Michael Maconachie, p. 13(t);
/Robert Pickett, pp. 12(t), 17, 18(t), 22, 27(crt); /Alan Towse, p. 27(tr); /Ken Wilson, pp. 13(b), 15. FLPA: /M.J.Thomas, p. 11(b).
Holt Studios: /Richard Anthony, p. 9(b); /Nigel Cattlin, pp. 9(t), 10(l), 11(t). NHPA: /Daniel Heuchin, pp. 19, 27(cl).
Photofusion: /Ute Klaphake, p. 24(tr); /Clariss Leahy, p. 25(b); /Bob Watkins, pp. 6, 7. Premaphotos: /Ken Preston-Mafham, p. 10(r).
Barrie Watts, pp. 12(b), 14, 27(tl).

The original publisher thanks the following children for modeling for this book: Donna Perkin, Nicholas Porter, Pernell Lamar Simpson.

Printed in Hong Kong

1 2 3 4 5 6 7 8 9 07 06 05 04 03

Life Cycles

Written by Peter Riley

Gareth Stevens Publishing
A WORLD ALMANAC EDUCATION GROUP COMPANY

About This Book

Everyday Science is designed to encourage children to think about their everyday world in a scientific way, by examining cause and effect through close observation and discussing what they have seen. Here are some tips to help you get the most from **Life Cycles**.

• This book introduces the basic concepts of life cycles and some of the vocabulary associated with them, such as hatching, changing, and growing, and prepares children for more advanced learning about life cycles.

• Encourage children to try Tom's activity on page 8. This activity can be linked to activities mentioned in **Plants**, another title in the **Everyday Science** series.

• On pages 9, 13, 15, 17, and 19, children are invited to predict the change in the life cycle of a living thing. Discuss the reasons for any answers children give before turning the page. For the question on page 9, look for an answer about flowers blooming. Children may also know that some buds produce leaves. On page 13, look for an answer about a butterfly climbing out. On page 15, children may say that people change. The butterfly and the frog provide examples of animals that have a complete change of form, instead of the more gradual changes seen in humans. On page 17, children may say that the tadpole comes out of the water. On page 19, children may refer to the butterfly, so use the images of the eggs to prompt them to talk about birds.

• If a child has a new, very young pet at home, you can suggest carrying out an activity similar to that described on page 23. Enlist the help of a parent or guardian to carry out Harry's activity. The data collected at home by a single student can be brought to school and used by the entire class to make a growth chart.

Contents

What Is a Life Cycle?

Every living thing has a life cycle. A life cycle is the set of changes that a plant or animal passes through from its beginning to its death.

An animal, such as a human baby, is born.

The baby grows.

He changes.

He grows and changes into an adult and can have young.

He grows old and will die someday.

Plants

The life cycle of a plant begins when its seed sprouts.

Tom puts some pea seeds in soil.

He waters them every day.

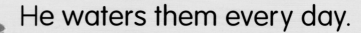

Soon, seedlings grow from the seeds.

The seedlings grow tall and become plants with leaves.

Tom plants them in his yard.

Buds grow from the plants.

What do you think will grow from the buds?
Turn the page to find out.

Flowers and Seeds

A flower grows from each bud. Flowers make a sweet liquid called nectar. Like some other insects, bees visit flowers to drink nectar.

Flowers also make pollen. Bees carry pollen from flower to flower as they drink the nectar.

Plants need pollen to make their seeds. The seeds scatter and grow into new plants.

Some plants die after the flowers make their seeds.

Some plants can grow new flowers and make seeds year after year.

A tree is a very large plant. Some trees live for hundreds of years.

Insects

An insect laid these eggs on a leaf.

Changes happen inside insect eggs.

Tiny caterpillars hatched from these eggs.

A caterpillar grows as it eats the leaf where it hatched. It changes into a pupa. The pupa spins a cocoon, or sac, around itself.

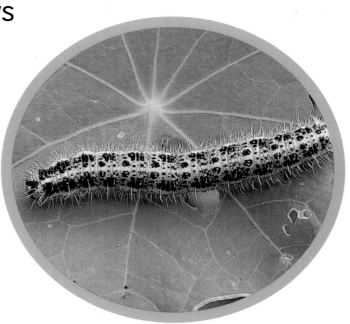

What do you think happens inside the cocoon?
Turn the page to find out.

A Butterfly

Inside the cocoon, the pupa slowly changes shape.

The cocoon splits open, and a butterfly wiggles out.

Like bees and other insects, the butterfly visits many different flowers to drink the nectar.

The butterfly lays some eggs. Shortly after laying its eggs, the butterfly will die.

What other animals change shape during their life cycles? Turn the page to find out.

Amphibians

Amphibians change shape during their life cycles.

Emily has some frog spawn from a pond. Frog spawn is a mass of frog eggs in a clear jelly.

You can see the black eggs in this frog spawn.

Emily checks the frog spawn every day. She sees the eggs changing shape inside the clear jelly. One day, she sees tadpoles hatching from the eggs.

The tadpoles grow and change shape. They slowly grow two rear legs.

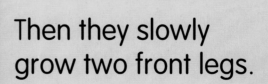

Then they slowly grow two front legs.

What change do you think happens next?
Turn the page to find out.

Frogs

The tadpoles' tails shrink. The tadpoles change shape and turn into baby frogs.

The baby frogs leave the water and live on land.

The baby frogs grow into adult frogs. After a few years, the adult frogs can make their own frog spawn.

Reptiles

The life cycle of a reptile begins with an egg. Snakes, turtles, and crocodiles are reptiles.

When a reptile, such as a snake, is fully grown, it can also lay eggs.

What other creatures begin their life cycles inside eggs? Turn the page to find out.

A bird begins its life cycle inside an egg.

Baby birds, called chicks, hatch from the eggs.

An adult bird must bring food, such as earthworms, to the chicks in its nest.

The chicks are soon ready to fly and find food on their own.

When the chicks are grown, they make nests and raise chicks themselves.

Mammals

A mammal has hair and drinks milk. Harry's cat, Tibby, is a mammal. She has six kittens.

The kittens feed on Tibby's milk. The milk helps them grow. Tibby drank her mother's milk when she was a kitten.

Harry weighs each kitten every week.
He records the weight of each kitten.

He picks out one
kitten and makes
a chart of its growth.
What do you think
the chart will show?

The kittens grow and change. They keep growing
and changing until they are about ten months old.
Then they become adult cats.

Humans

Here are some stages in the human life cycle.

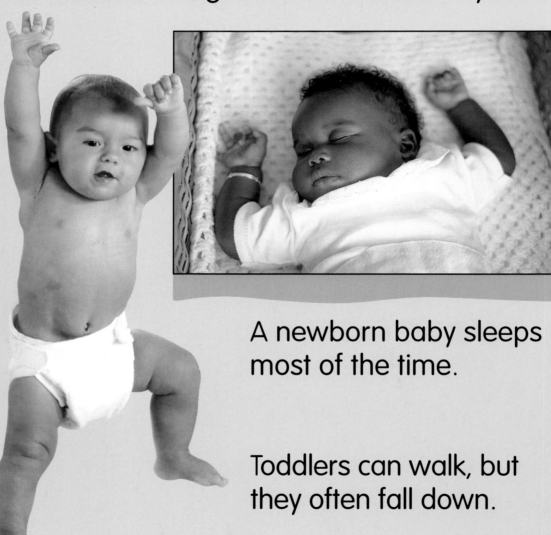

A newborn baby sleeps most of the time.

Toddlers can walk, but they often fall down.

Babies and toddlers need the care of an adult at all times.

Children begin to learn
to take care of themselves.

Adults take care
of themselves and
their children.

Are you a baby, a toddler, a child, or an adult?

Look at the pictures on the next page. What stage in the life cycle does each picture show?

Make your own table like this one and fill it in.

picture	starting out	growing up	having young
a			✔
b			
c			
d			
e			
f			
g			

a butterfly

b puppy

c reptile hatching
from egg

d tadpole

e bird

f seeds

g seedlings

Useful Words

amphibians: animals, such as frogs, toads, and newts, that start their life cycles in water but change into different body shapes before moving out of the water to live on land. Amphibians always return to water to lay their eggs.

buds: green lumps on stalks or twigs that can grow into flowers, leaves, or stems.

eggs: the first stage in the life cycles of animals such as birds and frogs.

frog spawn: a clear jelly holding a mass of frog eggs that will grow into tadpoles and then into adult frogs.

milk: the liquid food that baby mammals drink directly from their mothers.

nectar: a sweet liquid that plants make and that bees and some other insects and some birds drink.

pollen: a yellow powder that helps flowers make seeds.

pupa: a stage in a caterpillar's life after it stops eating and spins a cocoon and before it turns into a butterfly.

reptiles: a group of animals that hatch from eggs and that have scales on their skin. Some reptiles, such as snakes, have no legs and move by crawling on their bellies. Other reptiles, such as alligators, move using four short legs.

seedlings: young plants that have just started to grow from seeds.

Some Answers

Here are some answers to the questions asked in this book. If you had different answers, you may be right, too. Talk over your answers with other people and see if you can explain why they are right.

page 23   Harry's chart will show that the kitten's weight increases at a steady rate until it is fully grown.

page 25   You are probably at the child stage in the human life cycle.

page 26   a (butterfly) and e (bird) could have young. b (puppy), d (tadpole), and g (seedlings) are growing up. c (reptile) and f (seeds) are starting out. Sometimes an animal that begins its life cycle inside an egg uses the yolk for energy to help it grow and change. Seeds also store energy inside. A tiny plant inside a seed needs water to grow. The water helps split the seed open so that the seedling can grow up toward the sky while its roots grow down into the ground.

Conservation Note:

page 16–18 The frog spawn was removed from its pond for a very short time in order to take the photograph. If you plan to collect frog spawn, please consult a book on frogs or a wildlife expert to find out how to provide the proper care while the spawn is out of its natural environment. Make sure to return the spawn or tadpoles to the water where you found them to increase their chances of survival. An adult should help you do this.

For  More Information

More Books to Read

- *From Seed to Sunflower. Lifecycles (series)*
  Gerald Legg
  (Franklin Watts, Inc.)

- *Hummingbird. Life Cycles (series)*
  David M. Schwartz
  (Gareth Stevens Publishing)

- *A Tree Is A Plant.*
  Clyde Robert Bulla
  (HarperCollins)

Web Sites

- ANTS: Enchanted Learning
  www.zoomschool.com/subjects/insects/ants

- BrainPop: Metamorphosis
  *www.brainpop.com/science/plantsandanimals
  /metamorphosis/index.weml*

Index